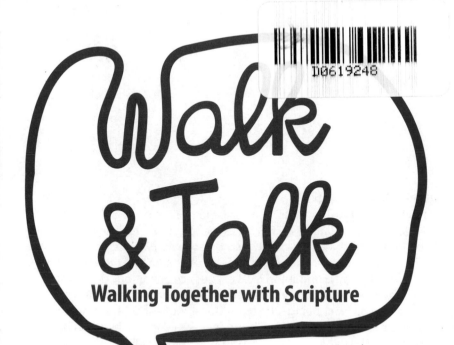

Walk & Talk

Walking Together with Scripture

Church Health
Memphis, TN

About Church Health

Church Health provides quality, affordable healthcare to uninsured working people and their families, and gives people tools to live healthier lives. Recognizing that health is more than prescribing pills, we also offer fitness, nutrition, and educational programming for children, teens and adults. Our Model for Healthy Living informs every service line of our organization and illustrates how the seven key dimensions of our health overlap and contribute to our overall well-being. Through local outreach and Church Health Resources, Church Health offers hope for a healthier life by reaching people where they worship and provides the support, consultation and education to start or strengthen health ministries in congregations. To support Church Health, visit churchhealth.org/donate/

Walk & Talk: Walking Together with Scripture
© 2011 Church Health Center, Inc. Memphis, TN

Updated Third Printing, 2017

ISBN: 978-1-62144-004-8

Printed in the United States of America.

Church Health is proud to produce this resource using recycled materials.

Written by Kira Dault and the wellness education staff of Church Health.

The primary objective of *Walk & Talk* is to help your community incorporate healthy habits into their lives of faith. Please feel free to copy and distribute this resource to aid your particular *Walk & Talk* program.

Contents

Introduction

About *Walk & Talk*:

Walk & Talk is a Bible study and devotional that is specifically designed to be used while you walk with a friend, with a member of your congregation, or by yourself. The primary objective of *Walk & Talk* is to help communities incorporate healthy habits into their lives of faith through physical movement and spiritual enrichment. Just as Jesus taught his disciples on the road, we believe that God speaks to us as we *Walk & Talk*.

How to Use *Walk & Talk*:

Walk & Talk is a year-long walking Bible study. While there are many options for using the resource, it is designed so that a group or pair of individuals could discuss a *Walk & Talk* devotional once a week for a full year. Each month has a different theme and provides 4 devotionals on that theme, for a total of 48 devotionals. There are also four optional devotionals provided at the back of the resource for a total of 52 devotionals, one for each week of the year. Each devotional provides a scripture passage, a short reflection, a series of discussion questions and a closing prayer.

Why Walk?

A Journey for Body and Spirit

Why should congregations get involved with walking programs? Our faith unites the body and spirit in a whole being. A walking program has physical benefits while also drawing us closer to God by adding an intentional reflective or devotional element. Stepping away—literally—from the demands of our daily routines to walk, reflect and pray reminds us that God created us and wants to come near to us.

Congregational walking programs don't have to be complicated: a few friends, choice of routes, a devotional resource, and a system for keeping track of progress are the basics. Walking as a spiritual practice invites us to enter into the lands of the Bible, bring body and spirit together, and experience greater well-being.

Church Health Reader EXCERPT
Visit chreader.org to read the entire article.

January
New Beginnings

In the beginning when God created the heavens and the earth, the earth was a formless void and darkness covered the face of the deep, while a wind from God swept over the face of the waters. Then God said, 'Let there be light'; and there was light.
—**Genesis 1:1–3**

This month, we will spend time considering the importance of new beginnings. In this creation story from Genesis, God creates structure out of chaos—marking the beginning of our world. Now we will consider how people of faith create structure out of chaos.

▶ Leader's Note

This month is geared toward the New Year and New Year's resolutions. If you are not using this for January, it can still be a good time for talking about goal-setting and healthy new beginnings.

New Beginnings: Week 1
New Year's Resolutions

And God saw that it was good. —Genesis 1:10b

Opening Thoughts

Most of us have made New Year's resolutions, but how many do we keep? God can help us to follow through when we set goals, and celebrates with us when we do follow through.

Discussion Questions

- What are the barriers that keep us from reaching our goals?
- Have you managed to keep a new resolution? What helped?
- What is a goal that you have for the New Year?
- What good thing is God doing in your life right now?

Closing Meditation

Lord, help us to remember the creation story, and to remember that you are the God who brings structure to chaos and shines light in dark places. Guide us and strengthen us in the New Year, and allow us to be a light for others. Thank you, God, for all good things. In your holy Name, Amen.

New Beginnings: Week 2
Health in the New Year

O Lord, by these things people live, and in all these is the life of my spirit. O restore me to health and make me live! —Isaiah 38:16

Opening Thoughts

The New Year is a wonderful time to consider our overall health and to set goals to improve our health. Our God is a God who restores our health. God gives us life, and life in abundance, and just as God restores our health, God calls us to care for our own health and the health of our communities.

Discussion Questions

- What are some ways you were healthier last year?
- What are some ways you want to be healthy this year?
- Healthy habits can include areas of diet and exercise, but we want to be spiritually healthy as well. What helps your body and spirit remain as healthy as possible?
- What good thing is God doing in your life right now?

Closing Meditation

Lord, thank you for the health we already have, and we pray that you would restore us to health and make us live a life of health. In your holy Name, Amen.

New Beginnings: Week 3
Change

- -

But, in accordance with his promise, we wait for new heavens and a new earth, where righteousness is at home. —2 Peter 3:13

Opening Thoughts

Some people embrace change, while many of us resist change as much as possible. But change is a part of life, and like other parts of life, sometimes change happens quickly, and sometimes it moves so slowly we miss it altogether. God guarantees change, but according to Peter, we must wait for it. This week, you will be asked to consider the challenges and blessings of change.

Discussion Questions

- How do you tend to deal with change?
- What kinds of changes have you experienced lately (changing seasons, hitting a "milestone" birthday, empty nest, school graduations)?
- What is a goal that you have for the New Year?
- What good thing is God doing in your life right now?

Closing Meditation

Lord, help us to bear witness to the new things that you are doing in our lives. Thank you for your presence and purpose. Help each of us to make the changes in our lives that we must make, and be with us when those changes become difficult. In your holy Name, Amen.

New Beginnings: Week 4

Encouraging Others

- -

Therefore encourage one another with these words.
—1 Thessalonians 4:18

Opening Thoughts

There is nothing like encouragement from a friend to put a smile on your face. Paul instructs us to encourage one another, as God encourages us. This week, you will be asked to offer support and encouragement for one another.

Discussion Questions

- Do you know someone who has set a goal for the New Year?
- How can you help a family member or a friend reach a particular goal?
- What kind of encouragement could you use this year?
- What good thing is God doing in the life of your family or congregation?

Closing Meditation

Lord, thank you for the encouragement we have received, and continue to encourage us as we move along the path toward our goal. Help us to share your support with those around us in our families and communities. In your holy Name, Amen.

February
Healthy Hearts

Create in me a clean heart, O God, and put a new and right spirit within me. *—*Psalm 51:10

This month, we will focus on developing healthy hearts, in body and spirit. We will explore the possibility that heart health can be an expression of faith. Our God is a God of clean hearts, and this month, we will work to experience that first hand.

▶ Leader's Note

This month is designed to focus on heart health. If you are using this curriculum in February, then you will encounter Valentine's Day. You can choose to use Valentine's Day as a focal point or not, but this would be an opportunity to encourage "healthy heart" behavior in place of chocolate and candy.

Healthy Hearts: Week 1
You Are What You Eat

You cause the grass to grow for the cattle, and plants for people to use, to bring forth food from the earth. —Psalm 104:14

Opening Thoughts

Better food habits can help you reduce your risk for heart attack. A healthful eating plan means choosing the right foods to eat and preparing foods in a healthy way. By choosing healthier foods we honor the body that God has given to us.

Discussion Questions

- Eating is a wonderful time for community and conversation. Who do you eat with most often? How might you improve your eating habits within your community?

- What healthy choices are you already making in your diet?

- What difference might it make in our eating habits if we remembered every day that our food is a gift from God?

- Healthy food choices will help your heart to be strong physically, but how can those same choices also make you strong spiritually?

Closing Meditation

Lord, make us mindful of how and where our food is grown, thankful for the people who plant and harvest our food, and for those who prepare our meals. Thank you for the gift of our bodies, and help us this week and from now on to keep our hearts as healthy as possible. In your holy Name, Amen.

Men, Women, and Children All Need Healthy Hearts

A new heart I will give you, and a new spirit I will put within you.
—Ezekiel 36:26a

Opening Thoughts

All people—male and female, young and old—need to keep their hearts as healthy as possible. We are all called to good stewardship of God's creation, which includes our bodies and especially our hearts.

Discussion Questions

- Heart disease is the leading cause of death of American women. Did you know this fact? Does it surprise you?

- Many times, we think that only older people need to pay attention to their health. Think of the children in your life. How can you encourage them to make healthy choices that will keep their hearts strong and healthy?

- Think of all the people you know: men, women and children. Do you think that your healthy choices can be a good example for them?

Closing Meditation

Thank you, God, for family and friends of all ages. Help us to be good stewards of your creation by caring for our hearts and the hearts of those around us. Make us all good ambassadors for heart health by helping us to make good choices for ourselves. In your holy Name, Amen.

Healthy Hearts: Week 3
Exercise and Fitness

You shall love the Lord your God with all your heart, and with all your soul, and with all your might. —Deuteronomy 6:5

Opening Thoughts

Swimming, cycling, jogging, skiing, dancing, walking and dozens of other activities can help your heart. Whether it is included in a structured exercise program or just part of your daily routine, all physical activity adds up to a healthier heart.

Discussion Questions

- What is your favorite kind of physical activity? How often do you do this activity?

- Do you prefer exercising alone or in a group?

- Exercising makes our hearts healthier physically, but it can also strengthen our spirits. How so?

- Many of us have responsibilities of caring for family members, and it can be difficult to make time for our own health. How does making time for your own good health also help those for whom you care?

Closing Meditation

Lord, make us mindful of the gift of our bodies and spirits each time we move today and throughout the week. Help us to celebrate our bodies by encouraging us to move and exercise. In your holy Name, Amen.

Healthy Hearts: Week 4
Maintaining a Healthy Weight

- -

Give us this day our daily bread. —Matthew 6:11

Opening Thoughts

Maintaining a healthy weight is important to our overall health. Many times we think of diets as giving up too much of the food we like to eat. Focusing on all of the good food that is both tasty and healthy can be a good way to start thinking about our diet.

Discussion Questions

- What is your favorite good and healthy food to eat?

- What is your favorite unhealthy treat? How often do you eat it? Are there any ways to change how you prepare this treat to make it more healthy?

- Think of a friend or family member with whom you share meals. What kinds of food do you enjoy together? What changes could you make to your meals to make them healthier?

Closing Meditation

Thank you God for the water that flows and food that grows. Help us to make healthy food choices. Give us guidance and strength, helping us to care for our bodies and to be as healthy as possible. In your holy Name, Amen.

March
Virtues for Healthy Living

By contrast, the fruit of the Spirit is love, joy, peace, patience, kindness, generosity, faithfulness, gentleness and self-control. There is no law against such things. And those who belong to Christ Jesus have crucified the flesh with its passions and desires. If we live by the Spirit, let us also be guided by the Spirit.
—**Galatians 5:22–25**

This month, we will reflect on the virtues for healthy living. In this passage from Galatians, Paul reminds us of the fruits of the Spirit, or the virtues for a healthy spiritual life and relationship with our Creator. As you move through the weeks to come, reflect on these fruits of the spirit and on how those fruits might help you on your journey.

▶ Leader's Note

This month often corresponds with the Christian Season of Lent, and though Lent and Easter practices are not mentioned explicitly in the reflections, there is a good deal of room to incorporate your church's Lenten observations into the month. (Think in terms of Lent being a time of penance and of spiritual discipline.)

Virtues for Healthy Living: Week 1
Patience

- -

Let the same mind be in you that was in Christ Jesus.
—Philippians 2:5

Opening Thoughts

Jesus was patient with his followers, especially those who were closest to him—his disciples. Even when the disciples did not get it—over and over again—Jesus was forgiving and patient. On our journeys to wellness, we can also remember to be patient with ourselves, just as Jesus is patient with us.

Discussion Questions

- What does patience mean to you?
- What does it mean to lose your patience? What kinds of things make you lose your patience?
- How can you be more patient with others? (Think of the way you can act with your friends, family and coworkers.)
- When we are trying to make healthy changes in our lives, it is sometimes difficult to stick with it. How can you be more patient with yourself?

Closing Meditation

Lord, give us patience. Help us to have patience with others when they do things we would not want them to do. Help us to have patience with ourselves when we do not make the kind of progress that we feel we ought to make. We pray that you would be with us, Lord, as we learn patience in our day-to-day lives. In your holy Name, Amen.

Virtues for Healthy Living: Week 2
Kindness and Love

He has told you, O mortal, what is good; and what does the Lord require of you but to do justice, and to love kindness, and to walk humbly with your God? —Micah 6:8

Opening Thoughts

This week, look at Jesus' kindness to those around him. He was kind to his disciples, but also to the strangers he encounters throughout his ministry. Jesus was willing to touch those who were untouchable, and to love all people, even those who rejected him. How can we embody love and kindness in our lives?

Discussion Questions

- What does kindness mean to you?
- Name a time when someone showed kindness toward you, and when you showed kindness to someone else.
- When is it difficult to show kindness?
- Name some ways that you can show kindness and love toward your body.

Closing Meditation

Lord, help us to be kind people. Let us remember to use kindness with others and with ourselves in everything we do. Let us also look for the love in our lives, sharing it with others and remembering it as we take care of ourselves. In your holy Name, Amen.

Virtues for Healthy Living: Week 3
Faithfulness and Hope

I declare that your steadfast love is established for ever; your faithfulness is as firm as the heavens. Let the heavens praise your wonders, O Lord, your faithfulness in the assembly of the holy ones.
—Psalm 89:2, 5

Opening Thoughts

This week, we look at faithfulness and hope, particularly our hope in God's faithfulness. In scripture, we are told and shown that our God is a faithful God. And God's faithfulness gives us hope, even when nothing or no one else can.

Discussion Questions

- What does faithfulness mean to you? What does hope mean?

- Talk about a time when you have struggled to find hope in a situation in your life. Did you manage to find it? How?

- Why is it important to keep hope in your heart?

- Name something that you hope for your own life, for your family and for the whole world.

Closing Meditation

Lord, you are faithful, and all of our hope lies in you. Help us to always keep hope in our hearts. As we struggle in the days and weeks ahead to make ourselves healthier in body, mind and spirit, help us to have hope along the way. In your holy Name, Amen.

Virtues for Healthy Living: Week 4

Gentleness

Come to me, all you that are weary and are carrying heavy burdens, and I will give you rest. Take my yoke upon you, and learn from me; for I am gentle and humble in heart, and you will find rest for your souls. For my yoke is easy, and my burden is light.
—Matthew 11:28–30

Opening Thoughts

This week we look to Jesus as an example of gentleness. Think, for example, of Jesus in the Gospel of Luke as he prays before his arrest. When he is arrested, Peter cuts off the ear of a servant of the high priest. But Jesus, declaring "No more of this!," healed the servant. Even in the midst of pain and violence, Jesus shows us a new way to be gentle.

Discussion Questions

- What does gentleness mean to you? Why is it important to practice gentleness?

- What are some ways that you can show gentleness to the people and things around you?

- How can you use gentleness in caring for your own body and spirit?

Closing Meditation

Lord, help us strive to be gentle in our actions and our words and with all of the people and things we encounter. Let us be gentle creatures in this world, doing no harm to our neighbors or our home on this earth. Let us also practice gentleness with ourselves, doing ourselves no harm, but striving to keep healthy and strong. In your holy Name, Amen.

April
The Abundant Life

I came that they may have life, and have it abundantly.
—John 10:10b

The emphasis this month is abundant living, which is promised by Jesus in the Gospel of John. This month, meditate on what abundant living means, and how we can embrace the abundant life that we have been promised.

▶ Leader's Note

TV Turn-Off Week falls in the month of April. The emphasis on abundant living this month could also be incorporated into discussions about TV Turn-Off Week, encouraging people to explore life's abundant possibilities, especially those outside the home—and away from the TV!

The Abundant Life: Week 1
Abundance in Body

I appeal to you therefore, brothers and sisters, by the mercies of God, to present your bodies as a living sacrifice, holy and acceptable to God, which is your spiritual worship. —Romans 12:1

Opening Thoughts

Our bodies are created and cared for by God. This week, we will think about how we can have more abundant life through the better care of our bodies.

Discussion Questions

- What does it mean to have abundant life through your body?

- We all have habits and patterns that prevent us from living into the abundance that God gives us in our bodies. What are some of those things for you?

- How can you celebrate your body, and the abundance of life available in your body?

- How can you encourage your friends and family to celebrate abundance in body? How can they encourage you?

Closing Meditation

Lord, help us to be mindful of the bodies that you have created for us. Help us to take better care of our bodies, and help us to celebrate our ability to move and to enjoy good food and breathe fresh air. Finally, help us to encourage one another to love and celebrate the abundant life that you give us through our bodies. In your holy Name, Amen.

The Abundant Life: Week 2
Abundance in Mind

Do not be conformed to this world, but be transformed by the renewing of your minds, so that you may discern what is the will of God—what is good and acceptable and perfect. —Romans 12:2

Opening Thoughts

In the passage above from Romans, Paul tells us to "be transformed by the renewing of your mind." In particular, this statement can give us hope, because it means that the habits that we have formed in our lives, that we may be "stuck" in, are, in fact, free to change.

Discussion Questions

- What does it mean to you to have abundant life with regards to your mind?

- What gets in the way of abundant life of the mind?

- How can you encourage others in your family, workplace or congregation to celebrate the abundant life of their minds? How might you be encouraged by them?

Closing Meditation

Lord, help us to encourage one another to be transformed by the renewing of our minds. Give us insight and endurance as we explore the habits of our minds, and as we make changes in our lives so that we might have more abundant life in and through you. In your holy Name, Amen.

The Abundant Life: Week 3
Abundance in Spirit

- -

Finally, beloved, whatever is true, whatever is honourable, whatever is just, whatever is pure, whatever is pleasing, whatever is commendable, if there is any excellence and if there is anything worthy of praise, think about these things. Keep on doing the things that you have learned and received and heard and seen in me, and the God of peace will be with you. —Philippians 4:8–9

Opening Thoughts

In this passage from his letter to the Philippians, Paul is imploring us to direct our spirits toward those things that are worthy of attention—the things that are of God. How can you and your community practice what Paul preaches?

Discussion Questions

- What does an abundant spiritual life mean to you?
- Name a time in your life when you felt abundance in spirit. Name a time when you did not feel abundance in your spiritual life.
- What can you do to live into an abundant spiritual life? Do you have habits that are getting in the way of living a spiritual life of abundance?
- None of us can live an abundant spiritual life alone. How can you help your community live a more abundant spiritual life?

Closing Meditation

Lord, help us to be mindful of your spirit throughout this week. Help us to spend our time and our energy putting into practice those things that are pure, admirable, lovely, excellent and praiseworthy. Help us to come together as a community, living an abundant spiritual life together. In your holy Name, Amen.

The Abundant Life: Week 4
Abundance in Life

Listen to me, O house of Jacob, all the remnant of the house of Israel, who have been borne by me from your birth, carried from the womb; even to your old age I am he, even when you turn grey I will carry you. I have made, and I will bear; I will carry and will save.
—Isaiah 46:3–4

Opening Thoughts

In this passage from Isaiah we are told that God knows us even before we are born, and God carries us and sustains us. In the previous three weeks, you have been asked to think about abundant life of body, mind and spirit separately. This week, you will be asked to think about the complete life in abundance, which includes body, mind and spirit.

Discussion Questions

- What do you think abundant life is? What does it include?
- In what ways do you embrace life in abundance? In what ways do you not?
- What can you do to better celebrate the life that you are given—in body, mind and spirit?
- The abundant life is not one that can be lived alone. How can your community more fully celebrate life in abundance?

Closing Meditation

Lord, we know that we are the work of your own hands. Help us to care for ourselves and our communities, to be stewards of your handiwork in us, and to live into the life abundant that you promise each of us. In your holy Name, Amen.

May
Diversity

For he [Christ] is our peace; in his flesh he has made both groups into one and has broken down the dividing wall, that is, the hostility between us. So he came and proclaimed peace to you who were far off and peace to those who were near; for through him both of us have access in one Spirit to the Father. So then you are no longer strangers and aliens, but you are citizens with the saints and also members of the household of God.
—Ephesians 2:14, 17–19

Throughout scripture, we witness a God of peace and of many nations. This month you will be asked to explore the challenges and benefits of diversity. How might diversity affect faithful living?

▶ Leader's Note

Diversity can be a difficult and challenging subject for many congregations. This term is often loaded with politically-charged language. We may be discouraged from using it, or we may overuse it without clear understanding of what the word means. Because of this challenge, it is all the more important to focus on this word "diversity" and what it means in our congregations.

Diversity: Week 1
What is Diversity?

There is no longer Jew or Greek, there is no longer slave or free, there is no longer male and female; for all of you are one in Christ Jesus.
—Galatians 3:28

Opening Thoughts

Diversity has become a buzzword in many settings, but what does it really mean? What does diversity mean for people of faith and for our relationship to God? Paul clearly understood that Jesus came for many kinds of people. This week, you will be asked to consider how diversity should function in the Church.

Discussion Questions

- What does the word "diversity" mean to you?
- What are some examples of things that can be diverse?
- How can people be diverse? In what ways are you part of a diverse population?
- Why does diversity matter, especially for people of faith?
- Is diversity in the Church a goal to be pursued? Why or why not?

Closing Meditation

Lord, help us all to recognize the diversity within your creation. We thank you for all of your good gifts, and help us to notice the beauty that comes with uniqueness and diversity. Help us to celebrate the differences that make us each unique. In your holy Name, Amen.

Diversity: Week 2
Being Different

- -

Do not be conformed to this world, but be transformed by the renewing of your minds, so that you may discern what is the will of God—what is good and acceptable and perfect. —Romans 12:2

Opening Thoughts

People are diverse in many ways: age, gender, race, religion, lifestyle, social and economic class, and physical ability, just to name a few. In the Psalms, we are reminded that each of us is fearfully and wonderfully made, and we are each made differently. These differences are all a part of God's wonderful creation.

Discussion Questions

- Think of your circle of friends. Are they mostly similar to you, or are there differences?

- Have you ever been singled out for being different? How did it feel?

- How do you respond to someone who is different, especially if they seem to feel alienated from the larger group?

- What are the challenges of getting to know someone who is different from you? What are the benefits?

Closing Meditation

Lord, help us to be mindful of the differences in your creation, especially when we are trying to get to know someone new. Help us to pay attention to those around us. Thank you for our friends, and thank you for the stranger in our midst. In your holy Name, Amen.

Diversity: Week 3

First Impressions

When Jesus came to the place, he looked up and said to him, 'Zacchaeus, hurry and come down; for I must stay at your house today.' So he hurried down and was happy to welcome him. All who saw it began to grumble and said, 'He has gone to be the guest of one who is a sinner.'
—Luke 19:5–7

Opening Thoughts

First impressions are important, but they are not always accurate. Many times, we pre-judge people before we get the chance to know them. Think about what might have happened if Jesus had judged Zacchaeus unworthy, just as everyone else had. Jesus had the generosity of spirit to give Zacchaeus more than a first impression.

Discussion Questions

- Though it's difficult to admit, how often do you judge people based on their appearance?

- Have you ever had a first impression about someone that turned out to be totally wrong? How did that make you feel?

- Has someone ever had a first impression of you that was wrong? How did you set the situation right, if you did?

Closing Meditation

Lord, help us look beyond superficial traits and first impressions to see people for who they really are. Help us to see the beauty and the goodness in all of your creation, and help us to honor every person as your beloved child. In your holy Name, Amen.

Diversity: Week 4

Words Matter

Indeed, the body does not consist of one member but of many. If the foot were to say, 'Because I am not a hand, I do not belong to the body', that would not make it any less a part of the body.
—1 Corinthians 12:14–15

Opening Thoughts

Many people resist the idea of "politically correct" language, but our words matter greatly. Words have the power to inflict harm as well as the power to heal. In the passage from Corinthians above, Paul reminds us that despite our difference (indeed, because of our differences), we are all part of one body in Christ.

Discussion Questions

- Have you ever been made fun of or called a name based on a physical characteristic? How did it make you feel?

- How do you refer to people who are sick? For example, would you say "a diabetic" or "a person with diabetes?" Do you think this could be an important distinction—especially for that person?

- We are often guilty of talking about people behind their backs. How can we be more mindful of showing love to our neighbors by speaking to them (and about them) with kind words?

Closing Meditation

God, help us to use uplifting and affirming language in our encounters with people of all colors, shapes and sizes. Help us to be mindful of the ways that we hurt as well as the ways that we can heal. In your holy Name, Amen.

June
The Fullness of God's Creation

God said, 'See, I have given you every plant yielding seed that is upon the face of all the earth, and every tree with seed in its fruit; you shall have them for food. And to every beast of the earth, and to every bird of the air, and to everything that creeps on the earth, everything that has the breath of life, I have given every green plant for food.' And it was so. God saw everything that he had made, and indeed, it was very good. —Genesis 1:29–31a

The emphasis this month is on the fullness of God's creation. As we reach the end of the spring and the beginning of summer, nature is blossoming, leaves fill the bare branches of trees, grass gets greener, flowers bloom. Everywhere we look, God's creation is full of color, warmth and light. This month is about celebrating the gifts from God the Creator.

▶ Leader's Note

At this beginning of the summer season, and halfway through our devotional, you might encourage your group to move to a different location as a way of experiencing the wideness of God's creation. Taking a "field trip" or "vacation" to a beach or outdoor walking trail can encourage your participants and make this summer month feel special.

The Fullness of God's Creation: Week 1
Sights

Consider the lilies of the field, how they grow; they neither toil nor spin, yet I tell you, even Solomon in all his glory was not clothed like one of these. But if God so clothes the grass of the field, which is alive today and tomorrow is thrown into the oven, will he not much more clothe you—you of little faith? —Matthew 6:28b–30

Opening Thoughts

When Jesus teaches his followers about God's care and concern for them, he uses flowers and grass as an illustration. By doing this, Jesus tells us that we can see God's love is visible in our surroundings.

Discussion Questions

- Talk about a time when you have seen God's care in your surroundings. Where were you? Did it make you stop and take notice? How did you feel?

- Even though we can say that God's care and concern is apparent in every aspect of God's creation, we don't always notice it. What gets in the way of you seeing God's care and concern?

- Jesus tells us that God's love and care extends even to the grass of the field. But Jesus also insists that God's love is very present in our own bodies. What are some ways that you can see and celebrate God's love for God's creation in the beautiful gift that is your own body and the bodies of all of God's children?

Closing Meditation

Lord, you have made the world a colorful and incredible place. Open our eyes so that we can see the goodness and bounty of your creation. Help us to celebrate the beauty in your creation and especially in our own bodies. In your holy Name, Amen.

The Fullness of God's Creation: Week 2
Sounds

Make a joyful noise to the Lord, all the earth. Worship the Lord with gladness; come into his presence with singing. Know that the Lord is God. It is he that made us, and we are his; we are his people, and the sheep of his pasture. —Psalm 100:1–3

Opening Thoughts

We are reminded of the sounds of God's creation throughout scripture. The Psalmist writes of the world shouting for joy. Even Jesus proclaims that even if the crowd were to keep quiet, the stones themselves would cry out! This week you will be asked to focus on the shouting, singing, buzzing and groaning of God's creation.

Discussion Questions

- Take one minute, get quiet and listen. What do you hear? Do you hear anything that you did not expect to hear?

- How do the sounds that you hear show and demonstrate the wonder and fullness of God's creation?

- As a part of God's creation, we are called to make a joyful noise unto the Lord. What are the sounds that you can make as an individual to celebrate God's creation?

Closing Meditation

God, you have made a noisy creation. Open our ears so that we might hear all the ways your care extends to your creation and to us. Help us to celebrate the fullness of your creation by listening to and participating in the sounds of your world. In your holy Name, Amen.

The Fullness of God's Creation: Week 3
Tastes

O taste and see that the Lord is good; happy are those who take refuge in him. —Psalm 34:8

Opening Thoughts

In this passage, the Psalmist writes that the goodness of God can not only be seen, but can actually be tasted. Recall that Jesus often spent time with his disciples and followers eating or enjoying food with them. This week, think about the ways that God's goodness is apparent in our food.

Discussion Questions

- When have you tasted God's goodness? What were you eating? Who were you with? What did it taste like?

- Think of the things that you have tasted this week. What have you tasted? What did you enjoy, and what did you dislike?

- Sometimes it is easy to take tastes for granted. What tastes have you taken for granted? Do you think that taking food (and tastes) for granted might lead to making unhealthy decisions about what you eat? Why or why not?

- What are some things that your community can do to celebrate the tastes of God's goodness?

Closing Meditation

Lord, thank you for all the tastes and the freshness of your creation. Help us to slow down and take notice of the great variety of tastes in the food you give us. In your holy Name, Amen.

The Fullness of God's Creation: Week 4
Smells

- -

…for now the winter is past, the rain is over and gone. The flowers appear on the earth; the time of singing has come,and the voice of the turtle-dove is heard in our land. The fig tree puts forth its figs, and the vines are in blossom; they give forth fragrance.
—Song of Songs 2:11–13a

Opening Thoughts

As spring turns to summer, there are all kinds of new scents as flowers bloom and leaves come onto the trees. This week, you will be asked to turn your focus to the smells of God's creation.

Discussion Questions

- Our lives are full of smells and fragrances. Do you have a favorite smell? A least favorite smell? What are they? What do they remind you of?

- Take a deep breath and pay attention to what you smell. Do you smell anything you expected to smell? Anything you did not expect to smell?

- How do smells communicate God's care and concern for creation? What are some ways that you can celebrate those smells?

- Each season has its own special smell. What kinds of smells do you expect to smell in the coming weeks? What do those smells make you think of?

Closing Meditation

God, we thank you for the ability to smell your creation, and for all of the fragrances that fill your world. Help us to take notice of and celebrate those smells, recognizing that the fullness of your creation includes fragrance. In your holy Name, Amen.

July
Walking Through the Valley

The Lord is my shepherd, I shall not want. He makes me lie down in green pastures; he leads me beside still waters; he restores my soul. He leads me in right paths for his name's sake. Even though I walk through the darkest valley, I fear no evil; for you are with me; your rod and your staff—they comfort me. **—Psalm 23:1–4**

Psalm 23 is often used at funerals and at times of death. But we can also look to this Psalm for encouragement. God gives encouragement even during times of difficulty. In our faith and in our life, we have to endure valleys of darkness. Psalm 23 assures us that as we walk those valleys, God walks beside us. This month, we will be focusing on persevering even when you find yourself walking through a dark valley.

▶ Leader's Note

If you are participating in the year-long *Walk & Talk* series, this month marks the half-way point. Since the middle can often be a difficult and discouraging place to be, this month can be used as an opportunity to address those difficulties that people may be facing at this half-way point, and also an opportunity to offer new encouragement.

Walking Through the Valley: Week 1
Discouragement

- -

When you pass through the waters, I will be with you; and through the rivers, they shall not overwhelm you; when you walk through fire you shall not be burned, and the flame shall not consume you.
—Isaiah 43:2

Opening Thoughts

In life, you will walk through fires and deep waters. At those times, life can be difficult, and it can be easy to become discouraged. But Isaiah assures us that there is no fire that we walk through where God will not be at our side. This week, you will be asked to focus on times when you have felt discouraged.

Discussion Questions

- What are some times when you have felt discouraged in your life? When have you felt the most discouraged?

- At times when you feel discouraged, how have you reacted in the past? Have you given up? Have you fought through?

- What are some healthy ways of dealing with discouragement? What are some unhealthy ways?

- It is sometimes easy to get discouraged when you are trying to make changes in your life. What are some of the ways that you can work through that discouragement?

Closing Meditation

Lord, help us to recognize that discouragement is, at times, a part of the process. Help us to cope with discouragement in healthy ways, knowing always that as difficult as the path may be, you walk with us. In your holy Name, Amen.

Walking Through the Valley: Week 2
Reconciliation

So if anyone is in Christ, there is a new creation: everything old has passed away; see, everything has become new!
—2 Corinthians 5:17

Opening Thoughts

In this passage, Paul is offering a reminder that Christ makes all things new. But in the midst of discouragement and difficulty, it can be hard to remember these things, and we feel distance from God rather than reconciliation. This week, you will be asked to reflect on the process of reconciliation, both with God, yourself and your community.

Discussion Questions

- What does reconciliation mean to you? When have you experienced reconciliation? (With God, with a friend or family member?)

- How do you think God works in the process of reconciliation?

- What old habits are you having a hard time breaking? Do you need to forgive yourself for those habits?

- How might God help you to forgive yourself? How might your community help you to forgive yourself?

Closing Meditation

Lord, help us to embrace the reconciliation that you offer us through Christ your Son. Help us to recognize that your reconciliation gives us the freedom to let go of old destructive habits and embrace new lives. In your holy Name, Amen.

Walking Through the Valley: Week 3
Continuous Conversion

That is not the way you learned Christ! For surely you have heard about him and were taught in him, as truth is in Jesus. You were taught to put away your former way of life, your old self, corrupt and deluded by its lusts, and to be renewed in the spirit of your minds, and to clothe yourselves with the new self, created according to the likeness of God in true righteousness and holiness.
—Ephesians 4:20–24

Opening Thoughts

Once again, Paul writes about becoming a new creation. Paul calls us to conversion in Christ, and this week, you will be asked to look at what that conversion might mean if we put it into practice everyday.

Discussion Questions

- What does conversion mean to you? Have you had any conversion experiences?

- We often think of conversion as a one-time, sudden epiphany. What difference would it make to consider conversion to be a continuous process?

- When we feel discouraged it can be easier to choose the "old self" instead of the "new self." How might you find a way to practice putting on the "new self" each day?

- What are the conversions that you are working on in your life? In your community?

Closing Meditation

Lord, help us to embrace the process of conversion—even when things are difficult. Assure us that we are being renewed through your grace and constant care. In your holy Name, Amen.

Walking Through the Valley: Week 4
Renewed Endurance

May the God of steadfastness and encouragement grant you to live in harmony with one another, in accordance with Christ Jesus, so that together you may with one voice glorify the God and Father of our Lord Jesus Christ. —Romans 15:5–6

Opening Thoughts

As we have considered this month, the path to life changes can be discouraging at times. But Paul reminds us that God gives us endurance and encouragement, both as individuals, and as a community.

Discussion Questions

- When you think of endurance, what do you think of? A race? Exercise? Perseverance?

- When have you had endurance? What did you accomplish? How did that feel? Did you have help or encouragement from someone other than yourself?

- What part of your life needs encouragement? Who might encourage you?

- Who do you know who might need encouragement today? How might you encourage them?

Closing Meditation

Lord, we thank you for granting us endurance and encouragement in times of trial. We pray that you would help us to accept encouragement when we need it and to encourage others. In your holy Name, Amen.

August
Community

Two are better than one, because they have a good reward for their toil. For if they fall, one will lift up the other; but woe to one who is alone and falls and does not have another to help. Again, if two lie together, they keep warm; but how can one keep warm alone? And though one might prevail against another, two will withstand one. A threefold cord is not quickly broken.
—**Ecclesiastes 4:9–12**

Ecclesiastes reminds us of the great strength of our relationships. When we join together, we are much more capable of achieving our goals and inspiring our communities. This month we will focus on the importance of relying on others for encouragement and reaching out to our communities.

▶ Leader's Note

In this month, many church ministries begin preparing for their fall programing. Depending on when you began *Walk & Talk,* this might be a good time to invite church members to join this walking ministry. Consider a public testimony or program, demonstrating to the community how this program has impacted the participants and inviting others to join in the fun!

Community: Week 1
Not Alone

We do not live to ourselves, and we do not die to ourselves. If we live, we live to the Lord, and if we die, we die to the Lord; so then, whether we live or whether we die, we are the Lord's. —Romans 14:7–8

Opening Thoughts

This month is largely about remembering that we are not alone on any of our journeys. In particular, this month, we acknowledge that making healthier choices and living healthier lives is easier to do when it is done in community. This week, you will be asked to reflect on the fact that we are all a part of a larger community.

Discussion Questions

- What are the different communities that you are a part of?
- What can you do to promote healthy living in these communities?
- How can your communities inspire you to make healthy choices in your life?
- Is there a community you would like to join, or have you fallen away from a community that you could re-engage?

Closing Meditation

Lord, make us mindful of the larger community around us. Help us to reach out beyond our comfort zone, remembering that you are active in the whole of the world. In your holy Name, Amen.

Community: Week 2
The Body of Christ

Now you are the body of Christ and individually members of it.
—1 Corinthians 12:27

Opening Thoughts

The Church can take a lesson from the way that God has put our bodies together. In this passage of Corinthians, we are reminded that each of us is a part of the larger whole. But just as we are all called to care for the body of Christ, so we are called to care for our physical bodies. This week, you will be asked to think about how we can care for our physical bodies as well as for the body of Christ.

Discussion Questions

- What does caring for your physical body mean to you? What does caring for the body of Christ mean to you?

- Who do you think is a part of the body of Christ?

- Do you think that caring for your body and caring for the body of Christ go together? Why or why not?

- How can you better care for your physical body? For the body of Christ?

Closing Meditation

Lord, thank you for caring for us, and for creating us in such a way that we are always a part of a larger whole. We pray that you would make us mindful of the bodies that you have given us, and that you would unite us in the body of Christ. In your holy Name, Amen.

Community: Week 3
Encouragement

- -

If then there is any encouragement in Christ, any consolation from love, any sharing in the Spirit, any compassion and sympathy, make my joy complete: be of the same mind, having the same love, being in full accord and of one mind. —Philippians 2:1–2

Opening Thoughts

We can find encouragement to live healthier lives by reaching out to the people around us. Paul reminds us in his letter to the Philippians that we can be encouraged by recalling Christ's love and fellowship. This week, you will be asked to think about being encouraged by and through your community.

Discussion Questions

- What kinds of encouragement do you receive? From your church? From your family? From God?
- What kind of encouragement do you give?
- Is there encouragement that you are not getting that you think you need? That your community needs?
- How can your community reach out and encourage others?

Closing Meditation

Lord, you have united us in Christ. Help us to be mindful of the encouragement that you give us, and help us to notice when those around us need encouragement. In your holy Name, Amen.

Community: Week 4

Sticking to It

And let us consider how to provoke one another to love and good deeds, not neglecting to meet together, as is the habit of some, but encouraging one another, and all the more as you see the Day approaching.
—Hebrews 10:24–25

Opening Thoughts

It is important, as we press forward, to have hope and maintain a vision of our goals. This week, you will be asked to consider how you and your community can continue to move forward toward the goal.

Discussion Questions

- What do you think is the goal of your community? What do you think the goal should be?

- Do you find it easier to accomplish goals as a part of a community or on your own? Why or why not?

- What are some of the habits that you have developed over the past several months that you would like to continue?

- Are there any habits that you would like to establish looking forward? Any habits for your community?

Closing Meditation

Lord, help us to be mindful of every step forward. Help us to keep perspective, to reach out for help when we need it, and to give help where it is needed. In your holy Name, Amen.

September
Back in the Swing of Things

Have you not known? Have you not heard? The Lord is the everlasting God, the Creator of the ends of the earth. He does not faint or grow weary; his understanding is unsearchable. He gives power to the faint, and strengthens the powerless. Even youths will faint and be weary, and the young will fall exhausted; but those who wait for the Lord shall renew their strength, they shall mount up with wings like eagles, they shall run and not be weary, they shall walk and not faint.
—Isaiah 40:28–31

During the course of this month, most children return to school. September is also a transition for many adults. The end of summer often means the end of vacations, of picnics, of long days and of porch sitting. This time of the year is often a time of transition, but we are reminded that God is with us in all walks of life—even the toughest changes.

▶ Leader's Note

As your ministry grows, think about new ways that you can introduce health ministries into your walking group or the wider Church. Is your group ready to take on a 5K walk or sponsor someone in a marathon? In this transition time try to find ways to grow and broaden your walking ministry.

Back in the Swing of Things: Week 1
Changing Seasons

- -

He changes times and seasons, deposes kings and sets up kings; he gives wisdom to the wise and knowledge to those who have understanding.
—Daniel 2:21

Opening Thoughts

This passage from Daniel reminds us that the changing of seasons and times is a part of God's creation. So even though there are times when transitions are tough, we rest in the assurance that God's hand is in the seasons and in the transitions. This week, you will be asked to think about the changing seasons and how the change might affect you.

Discussion Questions

- What are the major changes that you have noticed in the changing of the seasons?

- How do the changes make you feel? What are the good changes? The bad?

- Sometimes when seasons and schedules change, it becomes easy to neglect healthy habits in favor of easier, older habits. What habits have you fallen into, or what habits do you feel like you might fall into with the change of seasons?

- Where do you see God in the changing of the seasons? Where do you have a hard time seeing God as the world around you changes?

Closing Meditation

Lord, thank you for your hand in the changing of seasons, for the rising and the setting of the sun, and for the beauty of your creation. In your holy Name, Amen.

Back in the Swing of Things: Week 2
Fall Foods and Autumn Bounty

- -

God said, 'See, I have given you every plant yielding seed that is upon the face of all the earth, and every tree with seed in its fruit; you shall have them for food.' —Genesis 1:29

Opening Thoughts

This month, we are thinking about God's presence as the seasons change. Last week, we talked about how the changing of seasons are a part of God's creation. This week, you will be asked to think about how God provides for us throughout the changing of the seasons.

Discussion Questions

- When you think about the fall, what are the foods that you think of?

- What are some healthy changes that you can make in your diet this fall? How can you incorporate some of the fresh fall vegetables into your diet?

- What are the obstacles that you encounter to making healthy decisions about food?

- What are some decisions you can make that might help you to be a good steward of God's creation?

Closing Meditation

Lord, help us to see your care in the food that you provide for us. Help us to make healthy decisions, thus honoring your creation, and help us to slow down and enjoy the food that you provide this season, and all seasons. In your holy Name, Amen.

Back in the Swing of Things: Week 3
Goal Setting

- -

I press on towards the goal for the prize of the heavenly call of God in Christ Jesus. Let those of us then who are mature be of the same mind; and if you think differently about anything, this too God will reveal to you. Only let us hold fast to what we have attained.
—Philippians 3:14–16

Opening Thoughts

The transition from summer to autumn can be a wonderful time to make new goals or to revisit old ones. Here in his letter to the Philippians, Paul reminds us of the ultimate goal, and about living up to what we are given. This week, you will be asked to reflect on the goals that you currently have and on the goals that you might be making.

Discussion Questions

- Do you have any goals in your life? What are they?
- Do you have any health-related goals? Or spiritual goals? What are they?
- How might your health-related goals and your spiritual goals intersect?
- What support do you need from your community and how might you get it?

Closing Meditation

Lord, help us to set goals that help to give us more abundant life. You have given us our bodies and our spirits, so help us to keep our bodies and our spirits healthy, and to press on toward the goal. In your holy Name, Amen.

Back in the Swing of Things: Week 4
Looking Forward

-- -- -- -- -- -- -- -- -- -- -- -- -- -- -- -- -- -- -- --

My child, eat honey, for it is good, and the drippings of the honeycomb are sweet to your taste. Know that wisdom is such to your soul; if you find it, you will find a future, and your hope will not be cut off.
—Proverbs 24:13–14

Opening Thoughts

In the midst of transitions, we can occasionally lose sight of the good things that are coming and the hope that exists in the midst of transition. This passage from Proverbs reminds us of the wisdom that can be found in hope—looking forward is part of the faith that we share and a part of the message that Jesus brings us. This week you will be asked to look forward to this season and beyond.

Discussion Questions

- What are the things that you are looking forward to this season? What are you hopeful about? Where do you find fear?

- Do you ever lose sight of your hope for the future?

- What does a healthy and hopeful future look like for you? For your community?

- How can you and your community realize that healthy and hopeful future?

Closing Meditation

Lord, you offer us hope in the changing of the seasons and in all transitions. We pray today that you would make us mindful of that hope, that you would help us to have wisdom in the midst of all of our transitions. Help us to make healthy choices and to realize a healthy and hopeful future. In your holy Name, Amen.

October
Health and Hygiene

Even to your old age I am he, even when you turn grey I will carry you. I have made, and I will bear; I will carry and will save.
—Isaiah 46:4

God promises us that we are cared for, and that we will be sustained and carried. Isaiah tells us that even as we age, God will carry us. God cares for our bodies, and we can honor that care by caring for our own bodies. This month we will talk about the practical ways that we can honor God in taking care of the temples with which we have been blessed.

▶ Leader's Note

Healthy hygiene habits can seem mundane, but they are crucial for our bodies, particularly the elderly and the chronically ill. This month, find some ways to incorporate health information that might be beneficial for your church members. Focus on the importance of foot care for people with diabetes, or how someone with asthma can exercise softly. Use this month as a chance to once again broaden your health ministry.

Health and Hygiene: Week 1
Celebrating Your Health

Bless the Lord, O my soul, and do not forget all his benefits—who forgives all your iniquity, who heals all your diseases, who redeems your life from the Pit, who crowns you with steadfast love and mercy.
—Psalm 103:2–4

Opening Thoughts

In this passage, the Psalmist offers praise to a God who forgives sin and who heals diseases. The God that the Psalmist praises is a God who cares about the health of the body (heals diseases) and the health of the spirit (forgives sins). This week, you will be asked to think about how to celebrate the health that you have been given and how to offer praise to the God who cares for your whole person.

Discussion Questions

- What does "health" mean to you? Do you think immediately of physical health? Healthy food? Diets?

- When do you feel "healthy?" Are there times when you don't?

- When we feel sickness or disease, it can be difficult to remember to praise God for our health. What is one healthy part of your body that you are grateful for?

Closing Meditation

Lord, let us be thankful for the gifts of good health that we have, and let us continue to care for our bodies and work to improve our health everyday. Give us strength and patience to work through times of sickness or struggles in health. In your holy Name, Amen.

Health and Hygiene: Week 2
A Healthy Mouth

Then he [Jesus] called the crowd to him and said to them, 'Listen and understand: it is not what goes into the mouth that defiles a person, but it is what comes out of the mouth that defiles.'
—Matthew 15:10–11

Opening Thoughts

Dental health and hygiene is an important part of general health. So this week, you will be asked to spend some time reflecting on how your health choices affect your dental health. But in addition to considering the physical implications of how you care for your mouth, you will be asked to think about what comes out of your mouth—how our words can hurt or help our spirits.

Discussion Questions

- Why do you think it is important to keep your mouth healthy?
- What do you do every day to make sure your mouth stays healthy?
- How do you choose to use healthy words? What do you think that means?

Closing Meditation

Lord, thank you for giving us strong teeth, a powerful tongue and beautiful lips. Help us remember that what comes out of our mouths is often as important as what we put in them. Let us remember to choose to use healthy words. In your holy Name, Amen.

Health and Hygiene: Week 3
Keeping Our Spirits Healthy

If I speak in the tongues of mortals and of angels, but do not have love, I am a noisy gong or a clanging cymbal. And if I have prophetic powers, and understand all mysteries and all knowledge, and if I have all faith, so as to remove mountains, but do not have love, I am nothing.
—1 Corinthians 13:1–2

Opening Thoughts

It is sometimes difficult to remember that God creates each of us as entire persons. As a result, there are times when it can become easy to overemphasize one particular aspect of our persons. We can focus on healthy bodies, but if we neglect our spirits, then we are neglecting the whole person that God has created each of us to be. This week, you will be asked to consider the health of your spirit.

Discussion Questions

- What is your spirit? What does it mean to have a healthy spirit?

- Do you think your spirit is healthy? Why or why not? What things can you do to make your spirit healthy?

- What role do other people play in keeping your spirit healthy?

Closing Meditation

Lord, let us remember that our spirits are a part of the whole person that you have created. Make us mindful of our bodies and our spirits, and let us always be aware of the spirits of those around us so that we might love and protect them as well. In your holy Name, Amen.

Health and Hygiene: Week 4
Staying Healthy

But Jesus looked at them and said, 'For mortals it is impossible, but for God all things are possible.' —Matthew 19:26

Opening Thoughts

Being healthy and staying healthy is often difficult, and there will be periods of discouragement. But Jesus reminds us that with God's help all things are possible. This week, you will be asked to think about ways that you can stay healthy, and how God's care can help you to do that.

Discussion Questions

- Do you think you are a healthy person? If yes, how do you think you got to be that way? If no, how are you unhealthy?

- What are some healthy habits that you have? What are some not so healthy habits you have?

- How can you make a change to turn your not so healthy habits into healthy habits?

- Do you think healthy habits will help you to stay healthy? Why or why not?

Closing Meditation

Lord, we might take for granted the health that you have given each of us. Let us remember that it is our responsibility to keep our bodies healthy and strong. May we start to learn and develop healthy habits now to protect the gift of health that has been given to us. In your holy Name, Amen.

November
Your Wonderful Body

I praise you, for I am fearfully and wonderfully made. Wonderful are your works; that I know very well. My frame was not hidden from you, when I was being made in secret, intricately woven in the depths of the earth. Your eyes beheld my unformed substance.
—Psalm 139:14–16a

Each of us is fearfully and wonderfully made. Our bodies are created by God and have been "woven together." Sometimes it can be easy to lose sight of just how incredible our bodies are. We can get caught up in what we wish our bodies looked like, or with wishing we were younger or older or thinner. So this month, you will be asked to concentrate on the beautiful creation that is your body.

► Leader's Note

This month leads up to Thanksgiving and the holiday season. You could easily incorporate discussions of healthy holiday eating into your discussions this month, and provide some healthier recipe options for the Thanksgiving feast.

Your Wonderful Body: Week 1
My Favorites

Do not worry about anything, but in everything by prayer and supplication with thanksgiving let your requests be made known to God. And the peace of God, which surpasses all understanding, will guard your hearts and your minds in Christ Jesus.
—Philippians 4:6–7

Opening Thoughts

It is often easy to forget that your body was knit together by the Creator. This week, you will be asked to think about your body, to take a good look at it, and to rejoice in your favorite parts.

Discussion Questions

- How often do you celebrate your body? Do you ever have a difficult time celebrating your body? Why or why not?

- Why is that your favorite body part or parts? Talk about the things that you love about your body.

- How can you show God and others that you are thankful for that part of your body? For example, if your favorite part is your eyes, can you use them to read to other people who may not know how to read?

- Think about the inner workings of your body. Is there an organ or system that amazes you –the way our heal arches, or an intricate muscle, or how our skeleton is built?

Closing Meditation

Lord, thank you for the beautiful creation that you have given us in the form of our bodies. Help us to marvel at the intricacy and resilience that you have built into our very natures. In your holy Name, Amen.

Your Wonderful Body: Week 2
God Made You

So God created humankind in his image, in the image of God he created them; male and female he created them. God saw everything that he had made, and indeed, it was very good.
—Genesis 1:27, 31a

Opening Thoughts

Part of learning to celebrate your wonderful body is learning to believe that your body is created by God in the image of God. This week, you will be asked to reflect on the ways that God has shown God's love for all of us by creating our bodies in God's image.

Discussion Questions

- What does it mean to you to be "created in the image of God?"

- Can you see God's care for you in the way that your body is put together?

- Which body part would you really miss if you ever had to give that part up?

- Is there a part of your body that amazes you? Intrigues or confuses you?

Closing Meditation

God, we are thankful for the bodies that you have knit together for us. Help us to be mindful that each of our bodies is made in your image, and that we are a part of your wonderful and incredible creation. In your holy Name, Amen.

Your Wonderful Body: Week 3
Feeding Your Body and Spirit

Jesus said to them, 'Come and have breakfast.' Now none of the disciples dared to ask him, 'Who are you?' because they knew it was the Lord. Jesus came and took the bread and gave it to them, and did the same with the fish. —John 21:12–13

Opening Thoughts

After Jesus' resurrection, he makes a point to have a meal with his disciples. In fact, it is at the meals that his disciples recognize him and realize that he has risen from the dead. We ought to realize, therefore, that food is an important part of the life that we have been given. This week, you will be asked to reflect on the food that you give your bodies and spirits for nourishment.

Discussion Questions

- How does eating food help your body to stay healthy?
- Which foods do you eat that help your body have energy and strength?
- What foods do you believe your body needs more of?
- Just as your body needs to be fed, so your spirit needs to be fed. Can you think of a way to feed your spirit?

Closing Meditation

God, thank you for giving us food that is delicious and healthy to nourish our bodies. Help us to celebrate all of the food that you set before us, taking into our bodies that which will help us to rejoice in you and in our bodies, which you have created. In your holy Name, Amen.

Your Wonderful Body: Week 4
Thanksgiving

You have turned my mourning into dancing; you have taken off my sackcloth and clothed me with joy, so that my soul may praise you and not be silent. O Lord my God, I will give thanks to you for ever.
—Psalm 30:11–12

Opening Thoughts

Soon, we will celebrate Thanksgiving, and the holiday season will begin. During these times of celebration and family gatherings, it can become difficult to lose sight of healthy goals. This week, you will be asked to think about your Thanksgiving holiday, and how you can make it a healthy one.

Discussion Questions

- What are some of your favorite Thanksgiving foods to eat? What are some foods you want to eat during this season that are fruits and vegetables?

- When you sit down to eat, how can you make sure you do not overeat?

- After the meal, what could you do to help the day be a healthier day all around?

- What are the things that you are particularly thankful for this year?

Closing Meditation

Lord, thank you for all of the blessings you give us. Make us mindful of your gifts—the food on our tables, our beautifully made bodies, our communities. Be with us as we celebrate this week, and be with those who struggle to find reasons for thanks. In your holy Name, Amen.

December
The Gift of Health

Look, the virgin shall conceive and bear a son, and they shall name him 'Emmanuel', which means, 'God is with us.'
—**Matthew 1:23**

This month will be full of celebrations and Christmas songs. It is also a month likely to be full of anxiety about what gifts to buy, when to get what for whom, how to schedule yet another Christmas party. Here, however, you will be asked to reflect on the gifts that you have been given.

► Leader's Note

Consider how you might incorporate gift-giving in your group. Perhaps you might make small gifts for each other, collect funds to buy some good walking shoes for people in the community, or give the gift of testimony to the congregation, reflecting on how *Walk & Talk* has shaped your year.

The Gift of Health: Week 1
Surprises and Gifts

The angel said to her, 'The Holy Spirit will come upon you, and the power of the Most High will overshadow you; therefore the child to be born will be holy; he will be called Son of God. And now, your relative Elizabeth in her old age has also conceived a son; and this is the sixth month for her who was said to be barren. For nothing will be impossible with God.' —Luke 1:35–37

Opening Thoughts

It is probably safe to say that Mary did not expect to end up pregnant at the time the angel paid her a visit. And yet, the surprise was a gift. Sometimes in our lives, we receive surprises. This week, you will be asked to reflect on those surprises and gifts that we encounter in our lives both during the holiday season and at other times.

Discussion Questions

- Do you tend to like surprises? Why or why not?
- How does the holiday season make you experience a feeling of surprise or expectancy?
- When we celebrate the meaning of Christmas, we are celebrating God's gift of Jesus given to the world. How can we celebrate the gift of our bodies during this season?
- What kind of gifts do you like to give? What gifts do you enjoy receiving?

Closing Meditation

Lord, help us to embrace the surprises and gifts that come our way. Make us mindful that you entered the world in the most surprising way. Help us to give our bodies surprising and wonderful gifts during this holiday season. In your holy Name, Amen.

The Gift of Health: Week 2
Memories

And this is my prayer, that your love may overflow more and more with knowledge and full insight to help you to determine what is best, so that on the day of Christ you may be pure and blameless.
—Philippians 1:9–10

Opening Thoughts

The preparations for Christmas can be full of memories from childhood and beyond. Some memories are good and some are bad, but the holidays are wonderful times to make new memories and to begin new habits. This week, you will be asked to reflect on old memories and perhaps the creation of new ones during this holiday season.

Discussion Questions

- What is one of your favorite holiday memories?

- How can we think of memories as special gifts, especially during this time when we are celebrating the gift of Jesus Christ?

- Do you have any new memories you want to create this Christmas? How can you do that?

- What kind of "healthy" memory can you make this season?

Closing Meditation

Lord, thank you for the good memories that we have been given. Help us to survive the bad memories this holiday season, and help us to make new and healthy memories. In your holy Name, Amen.

The Gift of Health: Week 3
Sharing the Spirit of the Season

And you will say on that day: Give thanks to the Lord, call on his name; make known his deeds among the nations; proclaim that his name is exalted. Sing praises to the Lord, for he has done gloriously; let this be known in all the earth. —Isaiah 12:4–5

Opening Thoughts

This season is a season of gifts and gift-giving. During it we celebrate the gift of Jesus Christ given to us. This week, you will be asked to reflect on the ways that you can share the spirit of the season, and "let this be known to all the world."

Discussion Questions

- Why do you think it is important to have a healthy spirit?

- Just like we have talked about giving your body gifts during this season, how can you give your spirit gifts during this season?

- How can you share your healthy spirit with others during the holidays?

Closing Meditation

Lord, thank you for all of the gifts that you give us, and help us to be mindful of those gifts. Help us especially to embrace and share the spirit of this season of gifts and gift-giving. In your holy Name, Amen.

The Gift of Health: Week 4
The Greatest Gift

So they went with haste and found Mary and Joseph, and the child lying in the manger. When they saw this, they made known what had been told them about this child; and all who heard it were amazed at what the shepherds told them. But Mary treasured all these words and pondered them in her heart. —Luke 2:16–19

Opening Thoughts

As we approach Christmas, we can celebrate and embrace the greatest gift that God has given us. In addition to remembering those gifts that God gives us during this season, this week, you will be asked to reflect on the gifts that you can give to your body and to others during this season.

Discussion Questions

- What gifts did you give your body this holiday season?
- What healthy holiday memory did you make?
- How did you share a giving spirit to others this Christmas?
- What is the greatest gift you could give yourself this Christmas? What is the greatest gift you could receive this Christmas?

Closing Meditation

Lord, thank you for the gift of health that you have given us. Help us as we celebrate you in this season to celebrate the gifts that you give us each day. In your holy Name, Amen.

Optional
Leadership

My friends, if anyone is detected in a transgression, you who have received the Spirit should restore such a one in a spirit of gentleness. Take care that you yourselves are not tempted. Bear one another's burdens, and in this way you will fulfil the law of Christ.
—**Galatians 6:1–2**

Scripture is full of stories about people who became leaders in their communities. Sometimes they are reluctant or even destructive leaders, but others are very effective at leading their communities to a stronger and renewed faith. As leaders in our own communities, scripture calls us to ask what is leadership. How are we called to be leaders in Christ's Church?

▶ Leader's Note

This theme of "Leadership" is especially appropriate for church leaders—pastors, deacons, ministers and other church leaders. It may be especially helpful in encouraging many kinds of church leaders to speak about their own health and the leadership of their communities. If you are looking to lead *Walk & Talk* for a short-term gathering of church leaders (at a retreat, for example) these four weeks are a helpful tool.

Leadership: Week 1
What is Leadership?

- -

The gifts he gave were that some would be apostles, some prophets, some evangelists, some pastors and teachers, to equip the saints for the work of ministry, for building up the body of Christ, until all of us come to the unity of the faith and of the knowledge of the Son of God, to maturity, to the measure of the full stature of Christ.
—Ephesians 4:11–13

Opening Thoughts

Paul tells us over and over again that the body of Christ is made up of God's children. God calls some of them to be prophets, evangelists or pastors—that is, to be a leader in the community of faith. This week we will look at what leadership is and how leadership in the church is different from other kinds of leadership.

Discussion Questions

- What does it mean to be a leader?

- How are you a leader in your congregation? How are you a follower?

- Think of a church leader you admire. What skills or qualities do they possess? How do they live their life as a Christian leader?

- Who are the important leaders in your community? How is your leadership similar to theirs, and how is it different?

Closing Meditation

Lord, help us to remember the many ways you call us in your service and to keep in mind the challenges that leaders face. Strengthen the leaders of our communities that we may be faithful and fair in your service. In your holy Name, Amen.

Leadership: Week 2
Called into Leadership

And Mary said, 'My soul magnifies the Lord, and my spirit rejoices in God my Saviour, for he has looked with favour on the lowliness of his servant. Surely, from now on all generations will call me blessed; for the Mighty One has done great things for me, and holy is his name.'
—Luke 1:46–49

Opening Thoughts

As leaders in our churches, each of us has been called into God's ministry. It may come in a loud voice or in silence, in community or solitude, but each of us is uniquely called into ministry. This week we are asked to think about how we are called into God's service.

Discussion Questions

- What does it mean to be "called?" What specifically does it mean to be called into ministry in a congregation?

- How did you know you were called into leadership in the church? How do you tell the story of your call?

- Think of the many call stories from scripture—Abraham, Moses, Samuel, Ruth, Mary and others. What story do you remember the best? Which call story most resembles your own?

- Do you ever question your call? How do you handle doubts in your role as a church leader?

Closing Meditation

Lord, help us to remember that we are called by you into service in the church. Remind us of the cloud of witnesses that have heard your call and responded, and strengthen us when we are unsure of how you would have us work in the world. In your holy Name, Amen.

Leadership: Week 3
Being a Healthy Leader

- -

While they were worshipping the Lord and fasting, the Holy Spirit said, 'Set apart for me Barnabas and Saul for the work to which I have called them.' Then after fasting and praying they laid their hands on them and sent them off. —Acts 13:2–3

Opening Thoughts

The Holy Spirit called Barnabas and Saul to an important mission –and yet they did not go right away! The apostles knew that before they could complete their work they needed to fast and pray. They turned their attention to their bodies and their souls before they embarked on their mission. When we are called into leadership, we too have to pay attention to our bodies and our souls. This week we will consider what being a healthy leader means.

Discussion Questions

- When you are called to do something in Christ's service (like Saul and Barnabas), what kinds of practices do you do to prepare yourself?

- How are you a healthy leader? What changes or improvements have you made to your physical or spiritual health?

- Do you think that church leaders are more prone to unhealthy practices? Why or why not? What can you do to encourage healthy leadership in the church?

Closing Meditation

Lord, help us to remember we must prepare ourselves to be leaders in your church. Help us to practice healthy behaviors and take time to pay attention to our bodies and our spirits. In your holy Name, Amen.

Leadership: Week 4
How We Lead

He [Jesus] said to him the third time, 'Simon son of John, do you love me?' Peter felt hurt because he said to him the third time, 'Do you love me?' And he said to him, 'Lord, you know everything; you know that I love you.' Jesus said to him, 'Feed my sheep.' —John 21:17

Opening Thoughts

Peter is one of the most important leaders in the Church, and yet Jesus' command here is very simple. He does not command Peter to build a great cathedral, increase church attendance or even start a new program, but rather asks Peter—three times, in fact—to "Feed my sheep." As leaders, we have to discern when, where and how we will lead. Sometimes it may be in a public arena, and sometimes we may be called to leadership in a quiet way. This week we will think critically about how we lead.

Discussion Questions

- How do you practice leadership? Do you tend to lead by example? In your care to others?

- Think about a mentor or leader you admire. How do they practice leadership? How is your own leadership style similar or different?

- What are some of the characteristics of Jesus' leadership? How can you more closely emulate Jesus and how he leads others?

Closing Meditation

God, help us to discern how you would have us lead your communities. Remind us that there are many kinds of leaders, and challenge us to new and more effective ways of being a leader in your Church. In your holy Name, Amen.

Notes

Notes

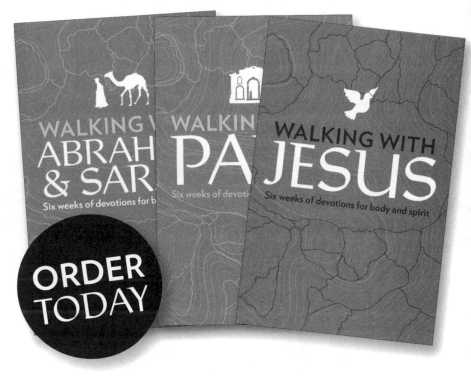